The Splendor of Forests

An Emma Rose Sparrow Book

Publish Date: November 12, 2015

Editor-in-Chief: Connor Chagnon
Sterling Elle Publishing
Bradford, Massachusetts

ISBN-13: 978-1519304469
ISBN-10: 1519304463

Photo Credits

The artist/source credits for the photos in this book are listed in the order in which they appear:

szefei/Shutterstock
LSaloni/Shutterstock
urciser/Shutterstock
djgis/Shutterstock
Jon Bilous/Shutterstock
Leonid Ikan/Shutterstock
Alexander Lukatskiy/Shutterstock
Inu/Shutterstock
gopause/Shutterstock
Ondrej83/Shutterstock
unchalee_foto/Shutterstock
urciser/Shutterstock
Bildagentur Zoonar GSmbH/
Cindy Creighton/Shutterstock
Ingrid Prats/Shutterstock
JOSE RAMIRO LAGUNA/Shutterstock
Takacs Szabolcs/Shutterstock
nitat/Shutterstock
RadVila/Shutterstock
Kotenko Oleksandr/Shutterstock
Robsonphoto/Shutterstock
Erik Mandre/Shutterstock

KPG Payless2/Shutterstock
Rolf_52/Shutterstock
Daniel Schiller/Shutterstock
WeStudio/Shutterstock
MarkMirror/Shutterstock
Carlos E. Santa Maria/Shutterstock
Daniel Caluian/Shutterstock
Matt Gibson/Shutterstock
Hector Ruiz Villar/Shutterstock
Olesya Kuznetsova/Shutterstock
rsooll/Shutterstock
Charles Knowles/Shutterstock
Lelechka/Shutterstock
Irina Bg/Shutterstock
Avramescu Florin/Shutterstock
David Havel/Shutterstock
Evgeny Kuzhilev/Shutterstock
Jakub.it/Shutterstock
Muskoka Stock Photos/Shutterstock
Orhan Cam/Shutterstock
Thomas Zsebok/Shutterstock
ANP/Shutterstock

33036481R00053

Made in the USA
Middletown, DE
10 January 2019